THE PROPHET AND THE BLIND MAN

Quran Stories for Little Hearts

by

S A N I Y A S N A I N   K H A N

Goodword**kidz**

Helping you build a family of faith

The Prophet Muhammad ﷺ used to sit near the Kabah and explain passages from the Quran to people.

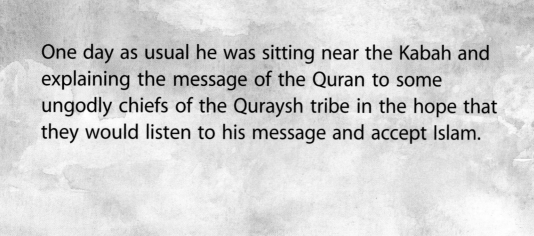

One day as usual he was sitting near the Kabah and explaining the message of the Quran to some ungodly chiefs of the Quraysh tribe in the hope that they would listen to his message and accept Islam.

As he was talking to the chiefs, a blind man whose name was Abdullah ibn Umm Maktum, approached him.

6

The blind man did not realize that the Prophet ﷺ was sitting with some high ranking people and was discussing some important matter with them.

9

As soon as the blind man
approached the Prophet,
he said, "O Messenger,
teach me about whatever
Allah has taught you."

The Prophet Muhammad ﷺ was annoyed at the blind man, cutting in like this and spoke roughly with him.

But Allah did not like the way the Prophet ﷺ responded to the blind man, who had come to seek guidance from him.

The following verses of the
Quran were then revealed
to the Prophet ﷺ :

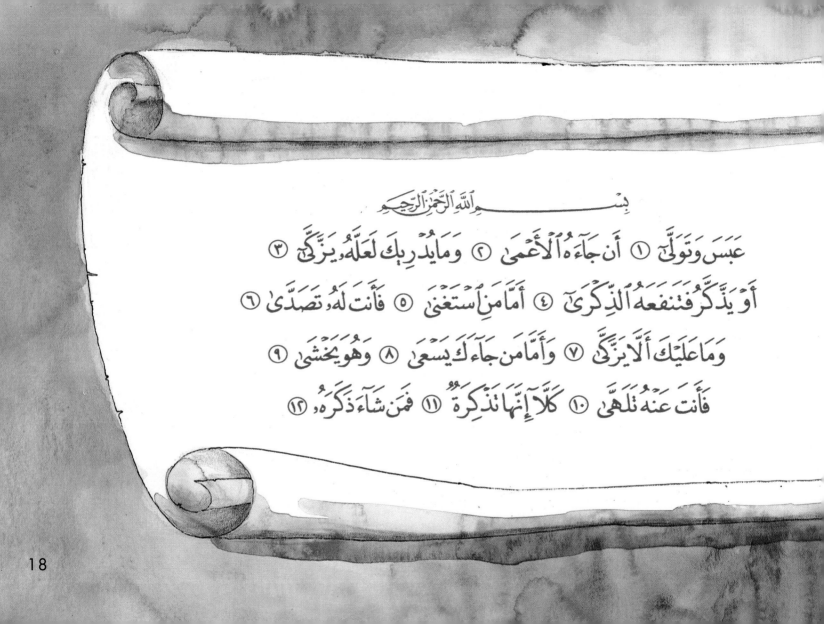

بِسْمِ اللَّهِ الرَّحْمَٰنِ الرَّحِيمِ

عَبَسَ وَتَوَلَّىٰ ① أَن جَاءَهُ الْأَعْمَىٰ ② وَمَا يُدْرِيكَ لَعَلَّهُ يَزَّكَّىٰ ③

أَوْ يَذَّكَّرُ فَتَنفَعَهُ الذِّكْرَىٰ ④ أَمَّا مَنِ اسْتَغْنَىٰ ⑤ فَأَنتَ لَهُ تَصَدَّىٰ ⑥

وَمَا عَلَيْكَ أَلَّا يَزَّكَّىٰ ⑦ وَأَمَّا مَن جَاءَكَ يَسْعَىٰ ⑧ وَهُوَ يَخْشَىٰ ⑨

فَأَنتَ عَنْهُ تَلَهَّىٰ ⑩ كَلَّا إِنَّهَا تَذْكِرَةٌ ⑪ فَمَن شَاءَ ذَكَرَهُ ⑫

When the blind man came to him, he (the Prophet)
gave him an angry look and turned his back on him.
Yet how do you know that he might purify himself?
Or be warned, and the warning may benefit him?
To one who was uncaring you were all attention,
although you do not have to ensure for it if he does not purify himself.
But one who comes to you eagerly and fearfully, you ignore.
No, indeed this (Quran) is a warning.
So, whoever is willing, let him seek remembrance from it.
(Surah Abasa, 80:1-12)

The Prophet Muhammad ﷺ later gave in, and treated Ibn Umm Maktum ever after with great respect, finally making him governor of Madinah.

21

The story of the blind man reminds us that no one in this world is superior to others, even if he has a high rank and position.

The message of this story is that one is only superior to another if he or she has a higher rank in the sight of the Lord.

Find Out More

To know more about the message and meaning of Allah's words, look up the following parts of the Quran which tell the story of the blind man.

Surah Abasa 80:1-12